Celebrate Around the World

by Margaret C. Hall

Scott Foresman
is an imprint of

Glenview, Illinois • Boston, Massachusetts • Chandler, Arizona
Upper Saddle River, New Jersey

Illustrations 19 Dan Trush

Photographs
Every effort has been made to secure permission and provide appropriate credit for photographic material. The publisher deeply regrets any omission and pledges to correct errors called to its attention in subsequent editions.

Unless otherwise acknowledged, all photographs are the property of Pearson Education, Inc.

Photo locators denoted as follows: Top (T), Center (C), Bottom (B), Left (L), Right (R), Background (Bkgd)

CVR (R) Getty Images, (L) © Jeff Hunter/Getty Images; **1** Blend Images/Getty Images; **3** (T) © Lindsay Hebberd/Corbis, (C) Chad Ehlers/Stock Connection/Digital Railroad, (B) ©A. Ramey/Photo Edit; **4** Blend Images/Getty Images; **5** © Justin Sullivan/Getty Images; **6** © Lindsay Hebberd/Corbis; **7** Getty Images; **8** ©Purestock/Alamy; **9** Chad Ehlers/Stock Connection/Digital Railroad; **10** © ISSEI KATO/Reuters/Corbis; **11** Muhammad Hamed/Reuters Media; **12** © Paul Barton/Getty Images; **14** © Jeff Hunter/Getty Images; **15** Brand X Pictures; **17** Kevin Fleming/Corbis; **s** Janis Miglavs/Danita Delimont Agency/Digital Railroad.

ISBN 13: 978-0-328-51417-5
ISBN 10:   0-328-51417-9

People all around the world celebrate special days. These special days are called holidays. People celebrate for many different reasons. Some holidays remind people about an important event from long

ago. Other holidays have a religious meaning or celebrate important days on the calendar.

People celebrate in many different ways too. Parades, feasts, gifts, and fireworks are just

some of the many ways that people celebrate. Holidays are important. They are times when families, friends, and communities come together.

Let's find out how people from different cultures celebrate!

During Cinco de Mayo, children hit piñatas to get the candy that is inside.

Parades and Parties

Parades are an important part of many celebrations, such as Cinco de Mayo, a Mexican holiday. The name of this holiday means "Fifth of May." That was the date in 1862 when the Mexican people won a **difficult** battle for their freedom against the French. Today Cinco de Mayo is a day of parades and parties. There are also speeches, dancing, and music.

During another holiday called Mardi Gras, there are so many parades and festivities that the streets in some cities look like a **circus**! Mardi Gras means "Fat Tuesday," and it always takes place the day before Lent begins. Lent is a religious season during which Christians prepare for Easter Sunday. Lent lasts for forty days.

During Mardi Gras there are parades with fancy floats decorated with **bouquets** of flowers and balloons. People on the floats throw beads, candy, and coins.

The day before Lent begins is celebrated in other places too. Brazil's Carnival celebration is a lot like Mardi Gras. There are parades, bright lights, and dancing in the streets. At midnight, the party ends and Lent begins.

It's fun to catch beads during a Mardi Gras parade!

Light

Candles, lights, and lanterns play a big part in many celebrations. One such celebration is the Hindu holiday, *Diwali*, which is known as the Festival of Lights. To celebrate Diwali, Hindus put candles and lanterns in their windows. Diwali is a celebration of the Hindu new year, which usually falls in October and November. In addition to lighting candles and lanterns, Hindus welcome their new year by painting their houses and wearing new clothing.

To celebrate Diwali, Hindu people paint beautiful designs on the walls of their homes.

One special candle is used to light the candles on the menorah.

Jewish people celebrate the Festival of Lights, or Hanukkah. Thousands of years ago, an important battle was won in Jerusalem. To give thanks, Jewish leaders lit a special oil lamp. According to the legend, there was only enough oil to keep the lamp burning for one day. But, amazingly, the lamp burned for eight days! Jewish people celebrate this miracle during Hanukkah.

The holiday lasts for eight nights to symbolize the eight nights that the oil lamp burned thousands of years ago. It usually begins in late November or early December. Jewish families light the candles on the menorah, a candleholder with nine candles. Each night, one candle is used to light the other eight. Some children receive gifts during Hanukkah too—one small gift each night.

Candles are important to the holiday of Kwanzaa as well. Kwanzaa is a festival honoring African American heritage. It focuses on the values of family, community responsibility, commerce, and self-improvement. Kwanzaa begins on December 26 and ends on January 1. Each night, family members light the black candle and one of the six other candles on a candleholder called a *Kinara*. The candles stand for the important principals of Kwanzaa such as creativity and faith. At the end of Kwanzaa, there is a big feast.

During Kwanzaa, every member of the family drinks from a special cup called a unity cup.

Winters are dark and very cold in Sweden. On St. Lucia's Day, lighted candles help people remember that the sun will return.

Another holiday in which light plays a central role is St. Lucia's Day in Sweden. St. Lucia is known as "the Queen of Lights." This holiday is celebrated each year on December 13, one of the shortest days of the year. On this day, a daughter, usually the oldest, gets up early in the morning before anyone else. She dresses in a white gown with a red sash and wears a crown of burning candles to represent the return of the sun. She wakes the family with special buns, coffee, and a song. Sometimes other children, both boys and girls, join in wearing white and carrying candles. Today battery-powered candle wreaths are worn.

Families and Feasts

Holidays are a special time for families to come together. The Japanese holiday called Children's Day is one example.

Children's Day is celebrated in Japan and in Japanese communities around the world. On May 5, families fly streamers shaped like fish. The fish stand for courage and strength. Children enjoy **nibbling** on favorite foods. They also make beautiful kites. The kites **soar** into the air over parks during the celebration.

Japan's Children's Day was once called Boy's Day. It was only for boys. But now it is a holiday for all children.

Eid al-Fitr is a happy time for Muslim children and families.

    Eid al-Fitr is an important holiday for Muslim families. This holiday takes place at the end of a month of prayer called *Ramadan*. During Ramadan, Muslims fast from sunrise to sunset. They don't eat or have even a **swallow** of water. During Ramadan, people read the Koran, a Muslim holy book. They also give money to the poor.

    Eid al-Fitr marks the end of the fasting. Everyone wears new clothing, and families say special prayers. Afterward, they have a big meal together. Sometimes there are carnivals with rides, games, and puppet shows.

In November, families in the United States come together to celebrate Thanksgiving Day. This holiday began hundreds of years ago. In 1620, about one hundred pilgrims from England settled in Plymouth, Massachusetts. Many came because they wanted to practice their religion in their own way. Almost half of these early settlers starved during that first winter in their new land.

The following year, the Native Americans helped the settlers grow more than enough food. In the fall of 1621, the settlers wanted to give thanks for the plentiful crop. They had a feast with the Native Americans that lasted several days.

Today Thanksgiving is a national holiday, celebrated the fourth Thursday of every November. Families give thanks and eat a big meal that often includes a turkey.

Most American families enjoy turkey for Thanksgiving Dinner.

Firecrackers and Fireworks

It wouldn't be Independence Day in the United States without fireworks! This holiday is held every July 4 all across the country. It celebrates the day when our nation gained its independence. Most towns and cities have big parades. Later, when it is dark, the skies light up with bright fireworks.

Fireworks light up the sky above the Eiffel Tower in Paris, France, on New Year's Eve.

Fireworks are used to celebrate many New Year's festivals. Celebrations to mark the new year are held all around the world starting on the last day of the year. For those who use the Gregorian calendar, such as the United States, New Year's Eve is December 31. The festivities often include a countdown to midnight, when fireworks are set off, to mark the exact moment that the new year begins.

Fireworks are also part of the Chinese New Year celebration. This celebration is one of the most important holidays for Chinese people around the world. It usually begins in January or February and lasts for fifteen days.

An old story tells why fireworks are part of the celebration. According to this story, a beast appeared at the end of the winter. The people were frightened. Then they learned that the beast was afraid of bright lights, loud noises, and the color red. They built a big fire and set off firecrackers. They also painted the doors of their homes red. All these things scared the beast away.

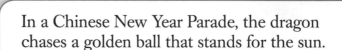

In a Chinese New Year Parade, the dragon chases a golden ball that stands for the sun.

There are parades during Chinese New Year too. A long dragon costume is worn by many people. One person controls the head while many others move the long body. They twist and turn through the streets. This dragon is made of silk or paper that has been stretched over wooden poles. When the parade is over, fireworks light the sky.

Fireworks help mark the beginning of the yearly Chinese Dragon Boat Festival. This summertime celebration started as a way to keep away evil spirits that cause sickness.

Today, cities around the world hold dragon boat races. People watch from a dock or **pier** as brightly painted boats race down the river. The front of each long boat looks like a dragon with an open mouth. A drummer stands in each boat and beats a drum during the race.

Dragon boats are ready to race in Portland, Oregon.

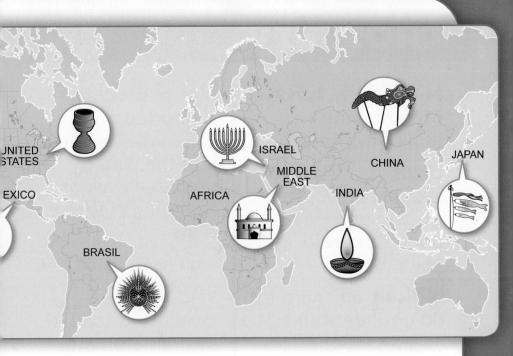

You now know about some of the holidays that people around the world celebrate. There are different customs and traditions that go along with each holiday. But one thing is the same–celebrations are a chance for people to come together and do something special, something they don't get to do every day.

Glossary

bouquets *n.* bunches of something, especially flowers

circus *n.* a traveling show of acrobats, clowns, horses, riders, and wild animals

difficult *adj.* hard to do or understand

nibbling *v.* eating with quick, small bites

pier *n.* structure supported on columns extending into the water, used as a walk or a landing place for ships

soar *v.* to fly at a great height

swallow *v.* to take into the stomach through the throat